Don't Hold Your Shit

Written By
Sydney Adeniyi

Illustrated By
Surajit Gupta

This is a work of fiction. Names, characters, places, and incidents either are the product of the author's imagination or are used fictitiously. Any resemblance to actual persons, living or dead, events, or locales is entirely coincidental.

Copyright © 2023 Sydney Adeniyi

All rights reserved. No part of this book may be reproduced or transmitted in any form or by any means, electronic or mechanical, including photocopying, recording, or by an information storage and retrieval system - except by a reviewer who may quote brief passages in a review to be printed in a magazine or newspaper - without permission in writing from the publisher.

To request permission, contact the publisher at dhys@thatguysydney.com

ISBN 979-8-9880397-2-3
ISBN 979-8-9880397-8-5 (pbk)
ISBN 979-8-9880397-3-0 (digital)

Written by Sydney Adeniyi
Illustrations by Surajit Gupta
Cover Art by Surajit Gupta & Sydney Adeniyi

Publisher website: www.dontholdyoursh.com

To my family, friends, and anyone who needs to let go.

Baby has to go, but Baby holds it in. It hurt before and Baby can't let go!

Don't hold your shit, you have to let go.
Baby says "No, no, no, I don't want to go!"

Holds shit in, squeezing head to toe!

Baby wants to share, but hurt-O! Baby hurts friends when they come close.

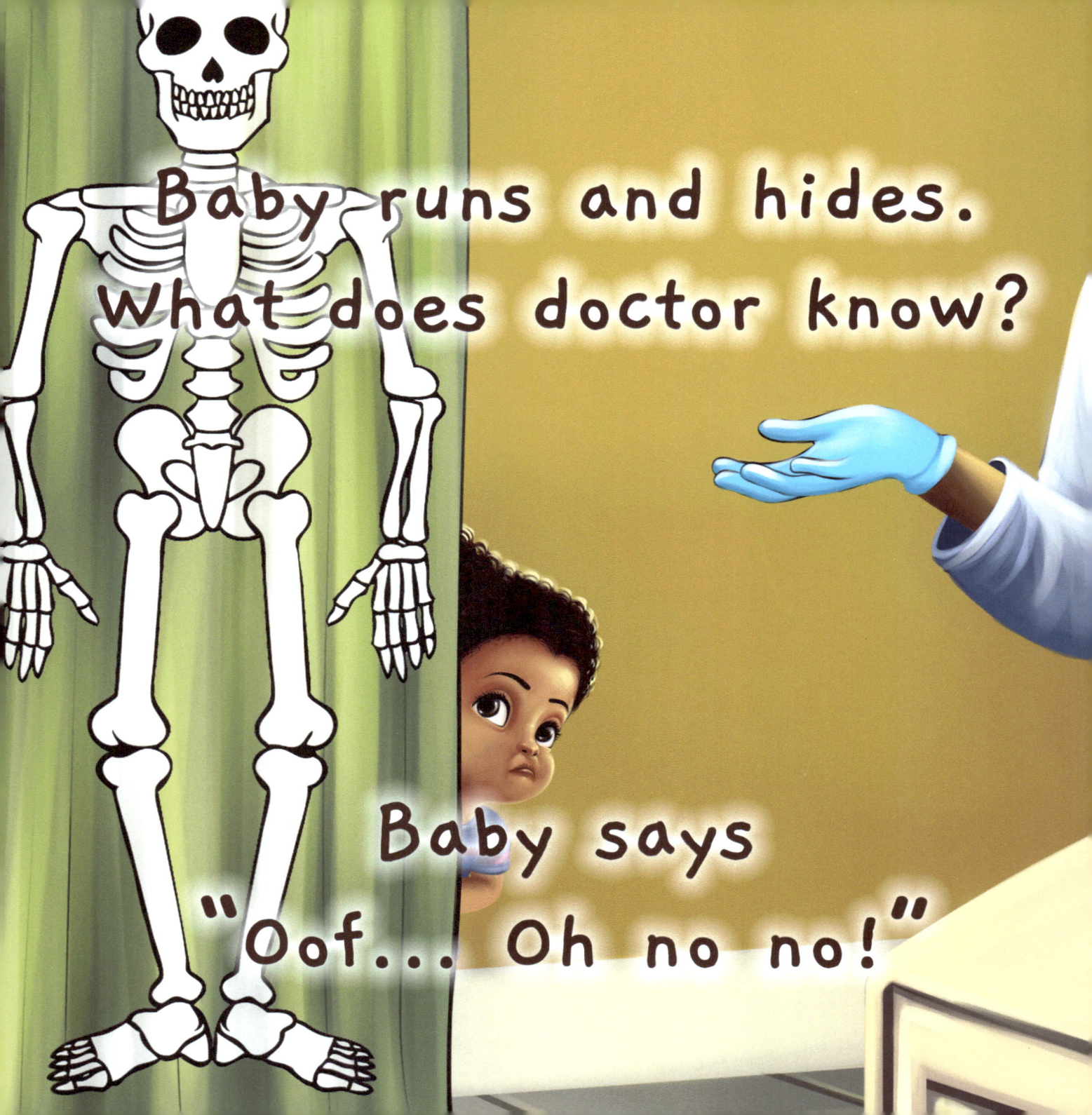

Sometimes hurt comes from friends, family, or food.

Baby says "No, no, nooo!"

Holds shit in...

but shit starts to flow.

Baby lets go...

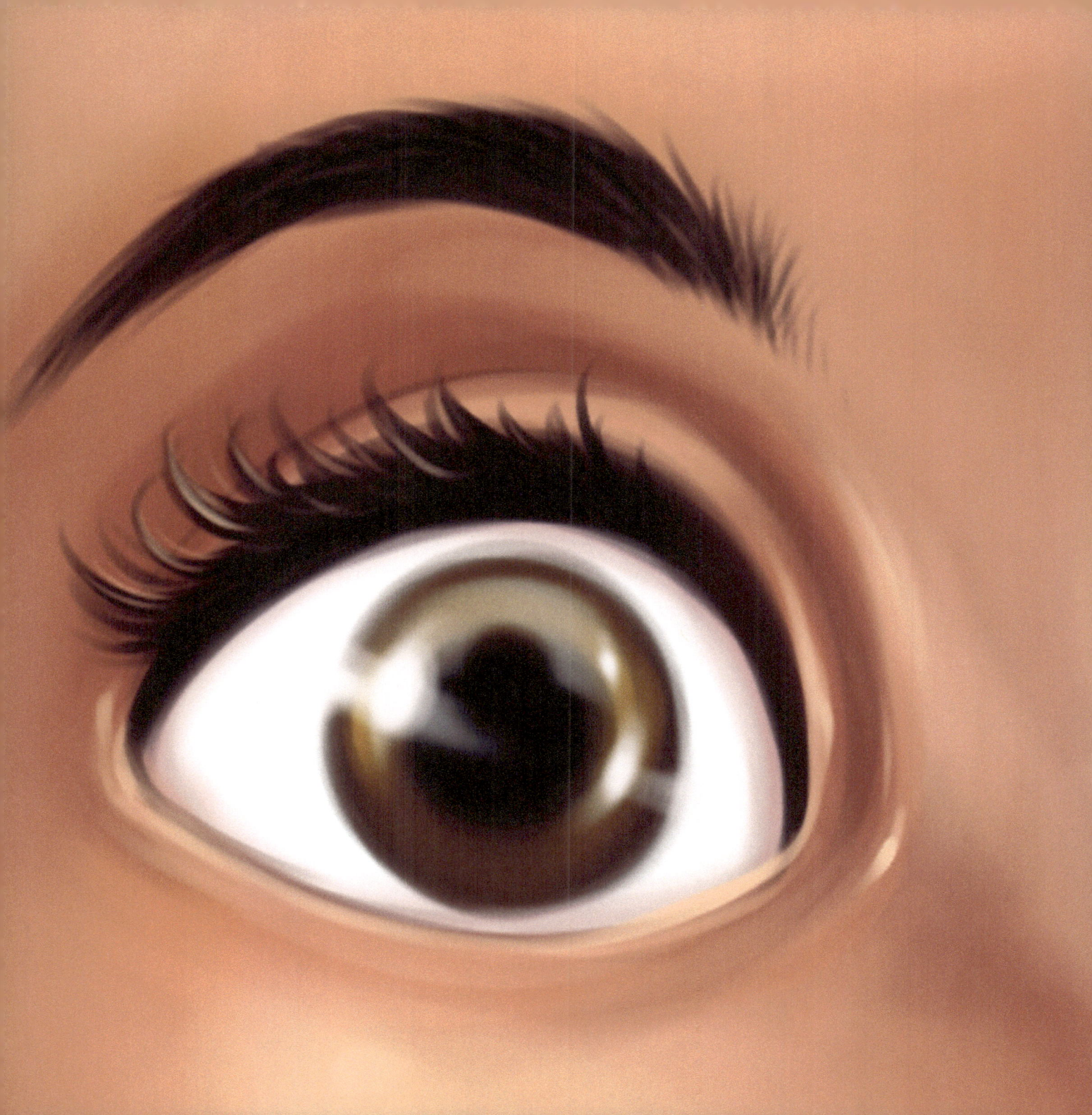

Letting go...

We all have shit: the resentment and pain we harbor from being hurt. For some reason, we hold onto it like a bad habit instead of letting it go like a silent but deadly fart in a crowded room. This hurt can come from anywhere: an ex leaving for someone younger, a job leaving for someone younger, a favorite restaurant leaving for somewhere younger... still, we hold onto these old pains of the past.

It seems logical to let go of shit bothering us, yet we play in it like a pig at a slop-n-slide. We're backed-up with the internalized fear of being hurt again. Or, we externalize it (sometimes unknowingly), acting out and hurting others. The fear of 'fool me twice' keeps us constipated with ___(fill in the blank)___ issues.

We've all been wronged by people, circumstances, or the corner of the bed we slammed our toe into. And yes, it's nice to identify the root cause (psst: it's usually the parents) but finding the culprit doesn't fix the damage. Being bullish on retribution begets more shit and a cycle of bullshit.

We can't be right holding on to all these wrongs. We have to let that shit go like our bodies' first-time reaction to foreign food. Be vulnerable, trust the lessons we've learned, so we can return to the right state of mind, by letting go...

About the Author

Sydney Adeniyi is a stand-up comic, actor, and writer who is passionate about mental health. He has worked for Big Brothers Big Sisters, volunteered at Head Start, and performed at colleges across the US. He is also a Laughter On Call comedian who fosters mental wellness and connection for both working professionals and memory care residents. Sydney's unique comedy writings encourage psychological safety, inclusion, and equity.

www.ingramcontent.com/pod-product-compliance
Lightning Source LLC
Chambersburg PA
CBHW040723060526
44119CB00083B/312